MW01274893

Seeds of a Nation

West Virginia

Margaret Coull Phillips

KIDHAVEN
PRESS™

THOMSON

GALE

San Diego • Detroit • New York • San Francisco • Cleveland
New Haven, Conn. • Waterville, Maine • London • Munich

THOMSON

GALE

Picture Credits

Cover Photo: © CORBIS
© Bettman/CORBIS 33
Chris Jouan, 37
© Christie's/ Images CORBIS, 12, 18
© CORBIS, 27
© David Muench/CORBIS, 16
© North Wind Picture Archive, 15, 17, 20, 21, 23, 26, 30, 32
© Peter Harholdt/CORBIS, 29
© Richard A. Cokke/CORBIS, 9
© Richard T. Nowitz/CORBIS, 25, 38
© N. Carter/North Wind Picture Archive, 8
© Stock Montage, Inc., 35, 36
© Underwood & Underwood/CORBIS, 31
© W. Cody/CORBIS, 6
© Werner Forman/Art Resource, NY, 10

© 2003 by KidHaven Press. KidHaven Press is an imprint of The Gale Group, Inc., a division of Thomson Learning, Inc.

KidHaven™ and Thomson Learning™ are trademarks used herein under license.

For more information, contact
KidHaven Press
27500 Drake Rd.
Farmington Hills, MI 48331-3535
Or you can visit our Internet site at http://www.gale.com/kidhaven/

LIBRARY OF CONGRESS CATALOGING-IN-PUBLICATION DATA

Phillips, Margaret Coull.
    West Virginia / by Margaret Coull Phillips.
        p. cm. — (Seeds of a nation)
    Includes bibliographical references and index.
    Summary: Provides a history of the thirty-fifth state to join the Union, from its earliest inhabitants, who are called mound builders, through the Civil War and its aftermath, plus a look at West Virginia today.
    ISBN 0-7377-1567-7 (hardback : alk. paper)
    1. West Virginia—History—To 1950—Juvenile literature. [1. West Virginia—History—To 1950.] I. Title. II. Series.
        F241.3 .P48 2004
        975.4—dc21

                                                                            2002152979

Printed in the United States of America

Contents

Introduction

The Mountain State

"Welcome to Wild and Wonderful West Virginia!" These are the words that greet many visitors as they enter the beautiful state of West Virginia. West Virginians are proud of their rugged mountains, swift rivers, and deep valleys. West Virginia is the only state that lies completely within the Appalachian mountain range. The Allegheny Mountains, a part of the Appalachian mountain range, are found in eastern West Virginia. The Appalachian *Plateau* lies to the west and makes up the rest of the state.

West Virginia borders Pennsylvania to the north, Maryland to the north and east, Virginia to the southeast, and Ohio and Kentucky to the west. West Virginia also has two panhandles; the northern panhandle is a finger of land that sticks up between Ohio and Pennsylvania, and the eastern panhandle lies between Maryland and Virginia. On a map West Virginia almost resembles a leaping frog.

Many of the rivers in West Virginia flow through the southern Appalachian Plateau. The Kanawha River flows west to the Ohio River. The Ohio River forms the boundary between Ohio and West Virginia, and the Potomac River is part of the boundary between West Virginia and Maryland. Most of the state's major cities are in the river valleys.

West Virginia was the thirty-fifth state to enter the union of the United States. It was a part of the state of Virginia until 1861. When the Civil War began in 1861, Virginia voted to **secede** from the United States and join the newly formed Confederate States of America. What was then western Virginia broke away from Virginia and remained within the union of the United States. It became an independent state on June 20, 1863. West Virginians

West Virginia's Place in the United States Today

Ohio

Pennsylvania

West Virginia

Kentucky

Virginia

Maryland

are proud of their unusual history and the part they played in preserving the union. In the years since statehood it has grown into an important state with industry, mining, and tourism. It truly is "wild and wonderful" and is perhaps, as singer John Denver wrote in his song about West Virginia, "almost heaven."

Nestled in the trees, this mill runs on energy from the Ohio River. Most of West Virginia's cities are located in the river valleys.

Chapter One

The Early People of West Virginia

Many years before the arrival of the Europeans and the settlement of what is now West Virginia, people had left their mark on the land. These first known people were called the mound builders. In the time before recorded history, a number of mound-building cultures built their mounds throughout the eastern woodlands and the Midwest.

The Adena People

The first of these mound builders, the Adenas lived in present-day West Virginia around the year 1000 B.C. **Conical** in shape, the mounds were built layer-by-layer over many years. When important people in Adena society died, they were buried in the mound along with **artifacts** such as bowls, jewelry, and tools. Then another layer of earth was added to the mound. Less important people were **cremated**, their ashes

The Adena, the first known people in West Virginia, buried important members of their society in giant mounds like the one pictured here.

placed in boxes made of logs, and then their bodies were added to the burial mounds.

Archaeologists have discovered much information about the Adena from excavating the mounds. Archaeologists know that the Adena were a tall people. Skeletons found in the mounds show that it was not uncommon for women to be six feet tall and for men to be nearly seven feet tall.

The Adena traded with other Native Americans over a wide area. Archaeologists found copper from the Great Lakes, mica from the Southeast, and shells from the Gulf of Mexico in the mounds. Other artifacts proved that the Adena were farmers, hunters, and fishermen. They wore copper and shell jewelry and played games. Around 100 B.C., the Adena culture began to die out. It was replaced by a new group of mound builders that became known as the Hopewell people.

The Hopewell People

Scholars think that the Hopewell culture grew out of the Adena culture. The Hopewell built larger and more elaborate earthen mounds. The mounds were built in a number of shapes, including squares, octagons, and circles.

The Hopewell people crafted animal figures like this mica bear. Many such figures have been discovered in their burial mounds.

The Hopewell used these mounds for ceremonies, as places to worship, and for social events.

Like the Adena, the Hopewell were traders. Along with the mica, copper, and shells that were common with the Adena, the Hopewell also traded with western tribes for a volcanic glass called obsidian, which was found in the Rocky Mountains. They used the obsidian to make tools.

The Hopewell hunted for bear, deer, small game, and the now extinct eastern woodland bison. They used every part of the animals, including the skins for blankets and clothing and the teeth and bones for tools, weapons, and for ornaments, jewelry, and clothing. The Hopewell also grew crops such as barley,

Hopewell artifacts like this pipe carved in the shape of a toad were used in ceremonies or to trade with other tribes.

squash, and sunflowers. They were adept at firing and decorating pots. Examples of their pots have been found in the mounds.

Historians think that the end of the Adena culture and beginning of the Hopewell culture was a peaceful process that went on for many years. No one knows just what happened to the mound builders. Some scholars think that disease killed them. Others think warfare or famine was to blame. They simply vanished, leaving their mounds and the artifacts they contained for archaeologists to find many hundreds of years later.

New Native Inhabitants

For quite a number of years after the disappearance of the mound builders, present-day West Virginia had few inhabitants. Archaeologists call this period in history the late prehistoric period. A few small, scattered villages existed mostly in the river valleys. Mainly, West Virginia was used as a common hunting ground by a number of tribes, chiefly the Iroquois Nation, which was centered in present-day New York state. The original Iroquois Nation was made up of five tribes: Mohawk, Oneida, Onondaga, Cayuga, and Seneca. Much later, in 1722, the Tuscarora joined with the other Iroquois tribes and they came to be called the Six Nations.

When the Europeans began to arrive in the new colonies in greater numbers in the 1600s, increasing numbers of Indians settled West Virginia. The Native Americans were being pushed westward by the pressure

Native Americans migrate west in search of a new home. As more Europeans arrived in the colonies, Indian tribes, were forced from their native lands.

of the European settlements along the Atlantic coast. The Indians were looking for new homelands because their traditional lands were being taken and settled by the Europeans. West Virginia became a haven for these displaced tribes. For example, after many years of wandering, the Shawnee found a home in the Ohio River valley. They would fight to keep this new homeland.

The mound builders of earlier times left a wonderful and interesting **legacy** on the land. New Native American settlements left a different history. The Native tribes that settled in West Virginia hoped to live undisturbed in their new surroundings. As the Europeans kept moving westward and starting new settlements, that dream of peace became impossible.

Chapter Two

Exploration and Its Consequences

When the Virginia colony was founded in the spring of 1607, there was little interest in exploring the land that lay to the west. The colonists were interested in getting the Jamestown settlement established and growing. The thickly forested mountains in the west also presented a barrier to exploration. Perhaps some of the earliest Europeans to see present-day West Virginia were the fur trappers and traders. Along with the hunters and trappers, the English sent lumberjacks into the woods to harvest the tall oak trees. These trees would be used as masts for the ships of the royal navy. No record was ever left of their travels.

In 1669, the Virginia colony sent a German doctor named John Lederer to explore western Virginia. He made three trips as he searched for a pathway through the Appalachian Mountains. He was the first European

A fur trapper hunts for game. Trappers and fur traders were the first Europeans to explore West Virginia.

to climb one of the highest peaks in western Virginia and look down into the Shenandoah Valley.

In 1671, the team of Thomas Batts and Robert Fallan reached the New River in southern present-day West Virginia. They were surprised to discover that the New River flowed to the west. All the other rivers they had encountered on their travels had flowed to the east. They claimed all the land that had rivers and

The New River meanders through southern West Virginia. In 1671, Thomas Batts and Robert Fallan claimed for England all land with rivers running into the New River.

streams that drained into the New River in the name of the English king. The amount of land that Batts and Fallan claimed for Britain was **vast**. This presented a problem in later years when the French also claimed much of the same territory.

In 1716, Lt. Gov. Alexander Spotswood led an unusual expedition into western Virginia. He took sixty men with him on horseback. His aim was to encourage western settlement. As they approached the mountains, they began to realize what a large and beautiful country lay to the west. When they returned home to eastern Virginia, they told stories about the wonderful land they had seen. Lt. Governor Spotswood gave a gift of a little golden horseshoe to each of the men who traveled with him. In present-day West Virginia, outstanding young students of West Virginia history are still given little golden horseshoes as a reward for their effort and scholarship.

The French Explorers

While the English explored the mountains of western Virginia, the French were busy exploring the Ohio River valley. The French established a colony in

Robert Cavelier de La Salle (standing) explores the Ohio River valley in a canoe manned by Indian guides. The French laid claim to West Virginia in order to monopolize the Indian fur trade.

present-day Canada that they called New France. From this colony they sent many explorers into the northern part of North America to claim as much land as possible in the name of the French king.

One of the most famous of these explorers was Robert Cavelier de La Salle. In 1669, he traveled with canoes and guides across Lake Erie and then overland to the headwaters of the Ohio River. His explorations gave France a strong claim to the Ohio River valley and western Virginia.

Another French explorer, Celeron de Bienville, made his way along the Ohio River in 1749. While he traveled he buried lead plates in the ground. These plates proclaimed that the land he explored belonged to France. He was hoping that these plates would bolster French claims to the Ohio River valley region.

As settlement moved westward from Virginia, English, French, and Indian traders came to together in outposts like this to trade fur, cloth, beads, and other items of daily life.

The French were not really interested in settling the land. They hoped to claim the land to keep fur trade with the Indians for themselves.

The Native Americans that were living and hunting in the area wanted to keep the Europeans out. They wanted to protect their hunting grounds and small settlements. However, the Indians had grown accustomed to the trade goods that they received for their furs. They could not make the iron kettles, steel hatchets, cloth, beads, and guns that they got in trade with the Europeans. Various tribes allied themselves with either the French or the English. The Iroquois tribes were traditional allies of the English, but they were also willing to trade with the French. The Shawnee, Delaware, Mingo, and several other tribes allied themselves with the French. These alliances and the fighting between the Native American tribes for the rich fur trade set the stage for a long and difficult conflict between France and Britain.

War Comes to the Mountains

It was not long after Celeron de Bienville buried his lead plates along the Ohio River valley that the French and Indian War began. This struggle between the British and the French for control of North America began in 1754. It was a bitter war that lasted for nine years. The British finally **prevailed** against the French, and the French were driven out of present-day West Virginia and the rest of the thirteen colonies.

British settlers prepare to attack French troops during the French and Indian War. When the war ended in 1763, the British had driven the French out of all thirteen colonies.

Once the war ended in 1763, many new settlers established homesteads in western Virginia, particularly in the river valleys. King George III of Britain tried to stem this tide of settlers by issuing a **proclamation** that forbade any new settlement west of the Allegheny Mountains. This proclamation was generally ignored, and new settlements continued to be established.

In addition, settlers treated Native Americans badly. The native tribes grew angry at the loss of their territory. In revenge, Indians began to raid the new settlements in an effort to drive the settlers back east of the mountains. It was a difficult struggle and resulted in tragedy on both sides.

A young colonist is pierced by an arrow during an Indian attack. Unwilling to surrender claims to the land of West Virginia, frequently Native Americans raided settlements there.

Finally, in 1768, the Iroquois signed a treaty with Britain. It was known as the Treaty of Fort Stanwix, named after a fort in present-day New York state. The Iroquois agreed to give up all their claims to the land between the Ohio River and the Allegheny Mountains. The Shawnee, however, did not agree to the treaty and refused to give up their claims to the Ohio River valley, so the strife continued for a number of years.

The early peaceful era of exploration of western Virginia ended with many painful conflicts and much bloodshed. Even after the American victory in the Revolutionary War in 1783, raids on the settlements and forts on the western Virginia frontier continued. Finally, the Indians were defeated by General Anthony Wayne at the Battle of Fallen Timbers in August 1794. The Native Americans gave up all their claims to western Virginia when they signed the Treaty of Greenville in 1794. This treaty led the way for the rapid settlement of present-day West Virginia.

Chapter Three

Following a Different Path

With the end of Indian raids in 1794, settlers poured into the northern and eastern panhandles of present-day West Virginia. The land in these areas was favorable to farming. Then the settlers slowly began to make their way over the mountains into central western Virginia. Many of the settlers were from Pennsylvania and Delaware. The majority were Scotch-Irish, Welsh, or German. Few of the settlers owned slaves, and many did not believe in slavery.

Settlers farm a plot of land. Crops like corn, beans, and potatoes and animals like chickens and pigs were staples of the settler's diet.

They did not have large landholdings like the plantations of the east. Instead, they farmed small plots of land in the valleys and on the hillsides. Their philosophy of life was vastly different from that of the settlers that lived in eastern Virginia.

The issue of slavery was becoming a difficult problem. Virginians began to be divided by the differences in their beliefs and lifestyles. As the gap between eastern and western Virginia widened, western Virginia was developing its own identity.

Life in the Early Settlements

Corn was the settlers' basic crop. They also planted squash, beans, peas, and potatoes. They harvested the berries and nuts that grew wild in the mountains. Along with the usual farm animals such as chickens and pigs, they hunted for game in the thick forests. The settlers ate venison, wild fowl such as turkey and geese, and even bear meat. Much of the meat was dried and preserved with salt. The settlers spent a lot of time making sure that they had enough **provisions** to last them through the long winter months.

The settlers' homes were built of logs. The cabins were small and had few windows. Most windows did not have glass but instead were covered with greased paper. The cabin usually had just one fireplace. The fireplace was used for cooking and also to provide heat for the family. Often there was a loft that was used for sleeping as well as for storing dried corn and other provisions.

Settlers in West Virginia built simple log homes like this one to provide shelter

Religion played an important role in the life of the early settlements. Church services would bring the settlers together. This was often the only socializing that the settlers had the opportunity to do. If the settlement did not have a church building, services would be held in the fields or in private homes. The minister was usually a "circuit-rider"—a preacher who traveled from settlement to settlement. Marriages and christenings had to wait until he arrived.

The early settlers of western Virginia **endured** many hardships. There were long, cold winters, Indian attacks, and land that was difficult to farm. But diseases were perhaps the greatest hardship. They could be more deadly than Indian attacks. Doctors were few and the

Rugged landscape and land that was difficult to farm were hardships endured by settlers in West Virginia.

pioneers had to rely on natural medicines made from roots, barks, and herbs. The settlers usually had large families because they knew that many of their children would not live to reach adulthood. A typhoid or diphtheria outbreak could kill an entire family very quickly.

Nevertheless, more settlers came to western Virginia. The population of western Virginia had expanded to almost eighty thousand people by the year 1800. Most of the people were farmers, but industry was also beginning to make its mark in the river valleys.

Early Industry

The first major industry in western Virginia was the salt industry. A salt spring near the Kanawha River was first used by the Native Americans to obtain salt. Salt water is called brine. The Indians would boil the brine in kettles to get the salt crystals that they needed to preserve their food. Later, the settlers used this same spring to obtain their salt. It became known as the "Great Buffalo Lick." Salt springs were often called "licks." In 1801, a well was successfully drilled to bring up salt brine that was trapped beneath the earth's surface. More wells were drilled, and western Virginia became one of the largest salt-producing regions in the new nation. Much later in West Virginia's history, these same salt deposits would be used in the chemical industry that fuels West Virginia's economy today.

In 1794, large deposits of coal were discovered in the mountains of central western Virginia. At first the coal was used mainly by the salt industry because large

Smoke billows from a nineteenth-century glass works in Wheeling, West Virginia. Large deposits of minerals in West Virginia allowed many different industries to thrive in the state.

amounts of it were needed to evaporate the water that was found in the salt brine. Most fuels such as wood and charcoal did not burn long enough to evaporate the brine water. Long-burning coal helped produce the salt crystals that were left after the water had evaporated. Eventually many other uses for the coal deposits were developed, and coal mining became the most important industry in western Virginia.

Iron ore was another mineral that was found in western Virginia. The production of iron grew to be an important industry. In 1794, a large iron plant was opened near present-day Weirton. It produced many tons of iron each day.

These minerals were in demand throughout the growing United States. It soon became evident that the lack of good roads was hampering the development of these early industries. Often the markets were far away from where the coal was mined or where the salt and iron were produced. The development of good transportation became a key to the future growth of western Virginia.

Roads and Railroads

Road building was difficult in the mountains. Tunnels had to be dug through the mountain ridges, and bridges had to be built over the many rivers and streams. Often roads were only Indian trails that connected isolated settlements. In 1806, a highway was begun at Cumberland, Maryland. This road was the first one to be built with government money. It was

Dawn lends a soft light to the Ohio River in this nineteenth-century painting. The many rivers and mountain ridges of West Virginia made it difficult to build roads.

called the National Road. The road was built for wagons and was used by the settlers moving west. It is now known as U.S. Route 40. This road was finally completed to Wheeling in 1818. It only went through a small slice of western Virginia, but it aided the growth of the city of Wheeling.

Another road that connected many towns and settlements in western Virginia was the Northwest Turnpike. It was completed in 1838, and it helped the towns and cities along its route to grow and prosper.

Railroads became another important element in the development of West Virginia. The first major railroad to be built was the Baltimore and Ohio. It took many years to complete the western Virginia portion because it was quite a task to build a railroad through the mountains and over the rivers in western Virginia. The railroad was completed to Wheeling in 1853.

The Chesapeake and Ohio Railroad was also important. It linked the Atlantic Ocean at Norfolk, Virginia, to the Ohio River in present-day Huntington, West Virginia. It was started before the beginning of the Civil War and was completed in 1873. These new railroads hauled coal, salt, iron, and other goods to distant markets. By the time of the American Civil War in 1861, western Virginia had grown from a region of small, scattered settlements to a region with

A wagon train makes its way over the National Road. The National Road and the Northwest Turnpike made travel and trade much easier.

The Baltimore and Ohio Railroad, pictured here, transported salt, coal, and iron to distant markets. Railroads enabled western Virginians to fully profit from their natural resources.

growing industries. The mountainous land in the west was rich in minerals, so mining and industry became more important than farming. The issue of slavery widened the gap between east and west. Many western Virginians worked to **abolish** slavery in Virginia. This was not a popular cause in eastern Virginia. When Virginia voted to secede from the Union in 1861 and join the Confederate States of America, Virginia would be split apart forever.

Chapter Four

A State is Born

Because western Virginia was growing and developing in a way that was different from the rest of Virginia, many of the people who lived in the western mountains began to feel that the government of the state did not respond to their needs. The Virginia Constitution, adopted in 1776, gave much of the power to the established eastern plantation owners and merchants. The people of western Virginia had little to say about the government of their state. Unless a

West Virginian children herd cattle. Unlike plantation owners in the east, most western Virginians farmed small plots of land.

man owned at least 25 acres of developed land or 50 acres of undeveloped land, he could not vote. Many western farms and homesteads were much smaller than 25 acres. The western Virginians could not compete with the large plantation owners in the east. In 1825, and again in 1829, conventions were held to address the concerns of the western Virginians. Many of the proposed reforms that would have benefited the small western farmers were voted down by the representatives in the Virginia General Assembly.

An African family is auctioned off at a slave market. Tension over the issue of slavery eventually led West Virginia to split from Virginia.

By 1829, the seeds of unrest were beginning to sprout in the western counties of Virginia. In 1850, another convention was held, and the right to vote was given to all white men in Virginia, even if they did not own land. This did help ease some of the **tension.**

The issue of slavery, however, was not settled. The nationwide debate over slavery was bringing the United States closer to civil war. Antislavery advocates often helped escaped slaves get to safety in Canada. Their southern owners felt that they should be returned. An attack on a government **arsenal** by antislavery forces at Harpers Ferry in present-day West Virginia angered many southerners. This was one of a series of events that contributed to the slide toward a very bitter civil war between the North and the South.

John Brown's Raid

John Brown hated slavery and believed that God had appointed him to bring it to an end. He planned to start a slave uprising. On October 16, 1859, John Brown and eighteen men raided the arsenal in Harpers Ferry and stole the guns and ammunition that were stored there. His plan was to give these weapons to the slaves in the hope that they would rebel against their masters. The raid failed, and John Brown was captured. He was tried for treason and hung by the state of Virginia. Because John Brown had been given money for the raid by antislavery supporters in the North, it caused a lot of resentment in

Harpers Ferry, the site of John Brown's raid, had a federal arsenal. An abolitionist, Brown attempted to steal the weapons and start a slave rebellion.

the South. John Brown had used this money to buy weapons for the attack. Many southerners considered the raid on the arsenal at Harpers Ferry as an act of war. Dark clouds began to gather over the nation.

Virginia Leaves the Union

Abraham Lincoln was elected president of the United States in November 1860. He had little or no support from the southern voters. Lincoln was anti-slavery. Once he was elected, many southern states began to leave the Union to form the Confederate States of America. In April 1861, Virginia held a convention that was called the Secession Convention. Many of the delegates that attended the convention were in favor of Virginia leaving the United States and joining the new Confederacy. When the

U.S. soldiers capture John Brown at Harpers Ferry, after Brown was tried for treason and hanged.

vote for secession was approved, the delegates from the western part of the state walked out of the convention vowing to establish a new state that was loyal to the Union of the United States.

In May and June 1861, the western delegates held two conventions in Wheeling. The delegates set up what they called the Restored Government of Virginia. A governor, United States senators, and representatives were chosen to represent the Restored Government of Virginia. Soon after the conventions met, President Lincoln recognized this government as the only government of Virginia. In

October 1861, the people of western Virginia voted for the creation of a new state. Another convention met in Wheeling in November 1861 to begin to write a constitution for this newly formed state. First they needed to choose a new name for the former region of western Virginia. The delegates proposed many names. After much debate and many compromises, West Virginia was finally chosen as the name of the new state.

Once the writing of the constitution was finished in February 1862, West Virginia applied for admission to the Union. Congress debated the matter until December 1862 and finally approved statehood. President Lincoln signed the West Virginia statehood bill on December 31, 1862. West Virginia was formally admitted to the Union on June 20, 1863.

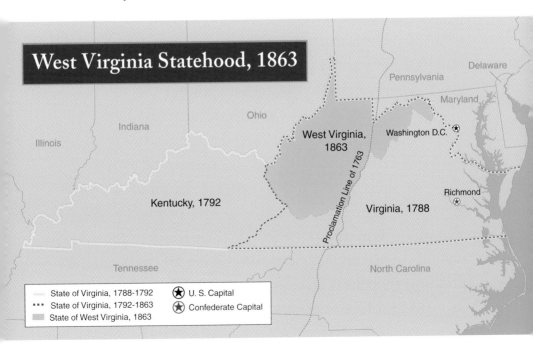

West Virginia Statehood, 1863

Delaware
Pennsylvania
Maryland
Ohio
Indiana
Illinois
West Virginia, 1863
Washington D.C.
Proclamation Line of 1763
Richmond
Kentucky, 1792
Virginia, 1788
Tennessee
North Carolina

— State of Virginia, 1788-1792   ★ U. S. Capital
••• State of Virginia, 1792-1863   ✪ Confederate Capital
▬ State of West Virginia, 1863

The process of becoming a state took several years and a lot of hard work. The people of the new state of West Virginia finally had a government that would be sympathetic to their needs.

The Civil War Aftermath

After the Civil War ended in April 1865, Virginia was readmitted to the Union of the United States. Virginia asked West Virginia to join with them once again and become a part of Virginia. The answer from West Virginia was a resounding no. A letter written by the West Virginia state legislature to the government of Virginia read in part: "The people of this state are unalterably opposed to reunion." West Virginia would follow its own path.

It would take some time before all the scars of war healed in West Virginia. West Virginia had contributed about thirty-two thousand soldiers to the Union armies and about ten thousand to the Confederacy. There was often bitterness among the veterans of both sides. At first Confederate veterans living in West Virginia were not allowed to vote. It was not until 1871 that they were finally permitted to have a voice in their government. African Americans were given the right to vote in 1872. The people of West Virginia eventually put their differences over the war behind them and became united in the process of building their new state. West Virginia was to realize its growth into a productive state with a place for all its citizens.

Present-Day West Virginia

West Virginia has continued to grow as an industrial state, with steel mills, ironworks, chemical plants, pottery works, and coal mines. But perhaps tourism is the biggest industry in West Virginia today. The spectacular scenery, beautiful rivers, rafting and canoeing, festivals, state parks, historical sites, hiking trails, and quaint villages continue to bring tourists year after year.

A hiker pauses to appreciate a West Virginia sunset. Known for its beautiful landscape, the state draws millions of tourists each year.

Facts About West Virginia

Population: 1,808,344

Land area: 24,282 square miles

Counties: Fifty-five

Size: Forty-first

Capital: Charleston

Became a state: June 20, 1863

Thirty-fifth state

Nickname: the Mountain State

State motto: Mountaineers Are Always Free

State animal: black bear

State bird: cardinal

State flower: rhododendron

State tree: sugar maple

Largest cities: Charleston, Wheeling, Parkersburg, Huntington, Morgantown, and Weirton

Rivers: New River, Greenbrier, Kanawha, Cheat, Tygart, Monongahela, Ohio, Potomac, and Tug Fork

Highest point: Spruce Knob, 4,862 feet

Early people: Adena, Hopewell, Shawnee, Cherokee, Delaware, and Mingo

Natural resources: coal, salt, oil, natural gas, iron ore, lumber, sand, stone, clay, and gravel

Glossary

abolish: Do away with, get rid of.

arsenal: A place where weapons are stored.

artifact: A man-made object from an earlier time.

conical: Cone shaped.

cremate: Burn to ashes.

endure: To patiently allow.

legacy: Anything handed down by an ancestor.

plateau: Elevated level land.

prevail: To have success.

proclamation: An official announcement.

provisions: A store or supply of food.

secede: To withdraw from a union.

tension: Strain.

vast: Great size.

Places to Visit in West Virginia

Moundsville: Grave Creek Mound, a prehistoric Adena mound

Harpers Ferry: Harpers Ferry National Historical Park

Weston: Jackson's Mill, General Thomas "Stonewall" Jackson's family farm

Bunker Hill: Morgan Monument, honors first white settler, named Morgan ap Morgan

Wheeling: Independence Hall–Customs House, and Oglebay Park

Beckley: Beckley Exhibition Coal Mine

Hillsboro: Pearl S. Buck Museum

Charleston: State Capitol Building, and South Charleston Mound, built by the Adena people

Petersburg: Smoke Hole Caverns; Native Americans used these caverns to prepare their meat for the winter

For Further Exploration

Books

Rodney S. Collins, *America the Beautiful: West Virginia*. Chicago: Childrens Press, 1994. This book presents an overview of the state's history, geography, people, and politics. It highlights many famous West Virginians and also the growing tourist industry in the state.

Tony Coulter, *La Salle and the Explorers of the Mississippi*. Philadelphia: Chelsea House, 1991. This is a detailed description of the life and times of René-Robert Cavelier, Sieur de La Salle. It covers the exploration of the Great Lakes and the Ohio and Mississippi River valleys by La Salle and other French explorers.

Terrance Dolan, *The Shawnee Indians*. Philadelphia: Chelsea House, 1996. The author presents a detailed look at the early Shawnee culture and also a lively retelling of the lives of some famous Shawnees such as Blue Jacket and the mighty chief Tecumseh.

Nancy Hoffman, *Celebrate the States: West Virginia*. New York: Benchmark Books, 1999. This is an interesting account of the story of West Virginia. It covers the history of the state as well as its geographical features. The book includes many maps and charts.

Patricia K. Kummer, *West Virginia*. Mankato, MN: Capstone Press, 1998. An easy-to-read book that gives a basic outline of West Virginia. It does not deal in depth with the state, but gives simple facts and information about the state's geography and tourism.

Sylvia McNair, *America the Beautiful: Virginia.* Chicago: Childrens Press, 1989. This book relates the story of Virginia from its founding as a colony to the present day. It touches on the geography, the government, the people, and the role of Virginia in both the Revolutionary War and the Civil War.

Kathleen Thompson, *Portrait of America: West Virginia.* Milwaukee: Raintree, 1988. This is a portrait of the people of present-day West Virginia, their occupations, and the economics of the state.

Websites

Burial Mounds (www.arrangements.com). This website gives a lot of information about the early burial mounds and the people who built them. It covers both the Adena people and the Hopewell culture and other mound-building tribes.

Life in a Log Home (www.campsilos.org). Although this website discusses life in a log home in Iowa, it can also relate to the lives of the early settlers of West Virginia. It provides a lot of detail about how our ancestors lived in early settlements.

Videos

Colonial Life for Children. Wynnewood, PA: Library Video Company, 1999. The information that is presented in this video is geared for children in the upper elementary grades. This information is presented in an interesting manner by both adults and children. The video discusses the early explorers, the first settlers, and the Native Americans.

Odyssey Myths and the Moundbuilders. Public Broadcasting Associates, 1987. This is an excellent reference video for the upper elementary pupil and also the classroom teacher. It gives a great deal of detail about the very early mound-building cultures.

Index

Index

About the Author

Margaret Coull Phillips is a retired elementary school teacher with twenty-five years of teaching experience. A graduate of Gwynedd-Mercy College, she also attended the University of Pittsburgh. Phillips grew up in the Pittsburgh area and has lived most of her life in Pennsylvania. The mother of four grown children, she enjoys visiting her grandchildren, camping, sewing, and gardening. Phillips lives in southeastern Pennsylvania with her husband, Richard, and their dog, Pretty.